# The Fairest Cape

## Cape Town and Environs

# The
# Fairest Cape

## Cape Town and Environs

BRIAN JOHNSON BARKER

STRUIK

Struik Publishers (Pty) Ltd
(a member of the Struik Publishing Group (Pty) Ltd)
Cornelis Struik House
80 McKenzie Street
Cape Town
8001

Reg. No.: 54/00965/07

First published in softcover 1991
First published in hardcover 1993
Second edition (softcover) 1994

Text © Brian Johnson Barker, 1991, 1993, 1994

Photographs © 1991, 1993, 1994 **Mark van Aardt** pages 1, 2/3, 5, 10/11,
12 (below right), 18/19, 20 (above left), 21, 22, 23, 24, 25, 26, 27, 28, 32/33, 34,
35, 36 (left), 37, 38/39, 40, 42, 44, 45, 48 (above), 49, 50, 51, 55 (above), 56/57,
58, 59, 66, 68, 70/71, 72, 74 (left), 80;
**Walter Knirr** pages 6/7, 20 (left), 23, 26/27, 36 (above), 41, 43, 47, 60 (left),
61 (right), 73, 77, 78/79;
**John Haigh** pages 8, 12 (above), 13, 14 (below right), 15, 16, 17 (above left),
31 (right), 46 (left), 48 (below);
**Ian Nienaber** pages 24 (above left), 55 (right), 60 (above), 76 (above and below)
**August Sycholt** pages 52, 53, 54, 62, 63, 64, 65, 67, 69, 75;
**Cloete Breytenbach** pages 17 (above), 74 (above);
**Ethel Rosenstrauch** page 14 (below).
**Roger de la Harpe** front cover
**Anthony Johnson** back cover

Cover design by Petal Palmer
Designed by Odette Marais
Typesetting by BellSet, Cape Town
Reproduction by Unifoto (Pty) Ltd, Cape Town
Printed and bound by Kyodo Printing Co (Pte) Ltd, Singapore

ISBN 1 86825 518 2

COVER *The sun setting behind
Table Mountain, one of the world's
most familiar landmarks, adds a sparkle
to the Victoria and Alfred Basin around
which the Waterfront (foreground)
has been built.*

FRONTISPIECE *Brightly painted bathing
cubicles at St James beach glow in the
early morning sunlight.*

TITLE PAGES *Table Mountain,
Cape Town's 'old grey mother', looks
down on the city with its architectural
mix from Renaissance-style City Hall to
the pepper-pot-like structures on the
mountain's lower slopes.*

OPPOSITE *Flowers and their sellers bring
brightness and breezy good humour to
their stand in Exchange Place.*

PAGES 6 & 7 *Dusk settles on the
'sunset coast' at Clifton, where still,
blue waters lap at empty sands.*

PAGE 8 *The upper cableway station
looms impressively out of cloud swirling
around the mountain top. Built by
Norwegian engineer Trygve Stromsoe,
the cableway has not had a single accident in over 50 years of existence.*

PAGES 10 & 11 *The rich red earth of
the Stellenbosch district is especially
noted for its crops of grapes that produce
excellent wines.*

BACK COVER *The magnificent homestead
at Groot Constantia, residence of
Governor of the Cape, Simon van der
Stel, until his death in 1712.*

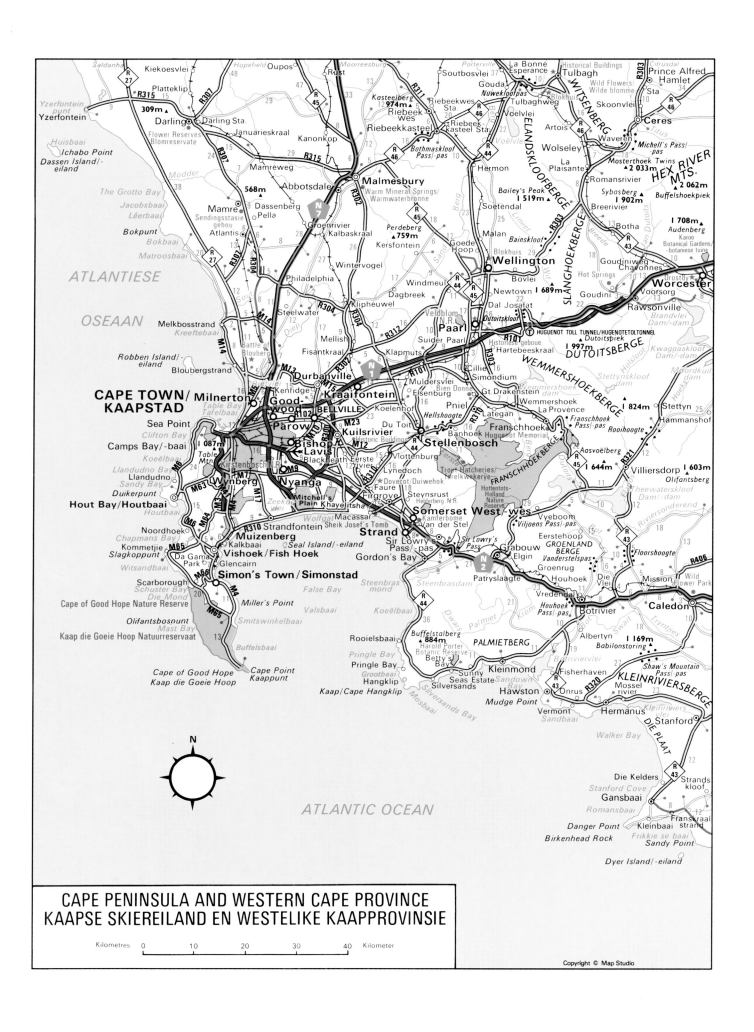

# CAPE PENINSULA AND WESTERN CAPE PROVINCE
## KAAPSE SKIEREILAND EN WESTELIKE KAAPPROVINSIE

Kilometres 0 10 20 30 40 Kilometer

# INTRODUCTION

ABOVE *Ornate plaster-work highlights a window from which a demure statuette surveys busy Long Street.*

BELOW RIGHT *St George's Street is now a pedestrian mall with cafes, stalls and entertainers to delight the leisurely visitor.*

It was the English navigator, Sir Francis Drake, who described the Cape of Good Hope as 'the fairest cape we saw in the whole circumference of the earth'. His description is apt for the whole of this southwestern corner of Africa although he saw just the Cape Peninsula from the deck of his little ship. Rarely wider than eight kilometres, the Peninsula stretches south from Mouille Point for some 56 kilometres to the tapering finger of Cape Point, which, tradition says, is the meeting place of the cold Atlantic and warm Indian oceans. Tradition is wrong, but any bather will confirm that the waters on the west, or Atlantic, coast are distinctly chillier than those of False Bay on the other side.

The most striking natural feature of the Peninsula is its chain of mountains, reaching its highest point of 1 087 metres at Maclear's Beacon on the famous Table Mountain. The bare rock-faces are composed of sandstone, deposited over millennia on a deep base of granite and shale. The gradual weathering of these components has produced a variety of soils, which sustain the world's smallest floral kingdom. The Cape Floral Kingdom covers a comparatively tiny strip of land along the south coast of South Africa, yet it contains a vast number of species. On the Peninsula alone grow over 2 600 indigenous species – more than in the entire British Isles. The common name for this vegetation is 'fynbos', a name derived from the narrow leaves of many of the plants.

It was an accident that brought permanent settlement from Europe – the running ashore in 1647 of a richly laden Dutch trading ship which was returning to the Netherlands from the East. Having salvaged the cargo, the sailors set up camp on the beach and waited to be taken off by the following year's trading fleet. They found they could grow vegetables as they did at home, and trade for cattle and sheep with the semi-nomadic tribespeople who periodically visited the shores of the bay. When they finally returned home, their report filled their employers, the Dutch East India Company, with enthusiasm, and Commander Jan van Riebeeck was sent to establish a refreshment station at the Cape, arriving in 1652.

A modest fort of mud and brick – its remains are now buried beneath the Grand Parade – was the start of the city of Cape Town. A more substantial fortress – the Castle of Good Hope – was begun in 1665, some 230 metres southeast of the fort, to be finally completed in 1679. The Castle still stands, and excavations and reconstruction have restored it to the height of its splendour, as it was toward the close of the 18th century. The visitor to the castle can find endless fascination in its dungeons and passageways, and admire the elegance of its cool museums and ballrooms, all contained within massive stone walls that, in the event, were never called upon to resist an enemy attack.

The nucleus of the city lies within the embrace of its mountains – Table Mountain, Devil's Peak, Lion's Head and Signal Hill forming an amphitheatre – and the sea that called it to life. The Company's Garden, where vegetables were once zealously sown and harvested, is a botanic garden today, but a centuries-old pear tree, surviving relic of the days of hardship, still faithfully puts out small, wizened fruit each year.

Among the concrete and glass of the modern city, gems of yesteryear can still be found, graced with gable and colonnade, and with floors of cool, dark slate quarried on Robben Island – the island of seals – that lies just off Cape Town's shores. There is the bright, white plasterwork of Koopmans De Wet House, with its lofty, cool and elegant interiors, and of the old Town House on cobbled Greenmarket Square where small-time vendors offer a bewildering array of goods from coins to clothing, pieces of old ships, books, jewellery and antiques. The Company's slave lodge was sited conveniently near the entrance to its Gardens, and over the years it changed both in appearance and in function. At one time the Cape colonial parliament met within its thick, white walls, and then, when the new Houses of Parliament had been built, it housed the Supreme Court. It stands today as the South African Cultural History Museum, just across narrow Bureau Street from the historic mother church of the Dutch Reformed faith in South Africa.

The city's street names tell their own story. Buitenkant, Buitengracht and Buitencingel marked the outer edges of the settlement less than 200 years ago. Strand Street and Waterkant Street are reminders that the sea was once much closer to the mountain. Many new hectares were won by filling in the bay, to create the foreshore area, and the statue of Jan van Riebeeck in busy Heerengracht stands close to the spot where he originally stepped ashore more than 300 years ago. His eyes of bronze are turned towards the massif of Table Mountain where, in the summer months, wisps of white cloud gather about the flat summit, or come tumbling down the steep flanks to dissipate in the warmer air of the lower slopes. This is the 'table cloth', laid by the southeast wind that early Capetonians called 'the Cape doctor' because, they said, it swept all dirt and disease far out to sea. When the wind is not blowing too strongly, you will see the tiny shapes of the cable cars that ferry thousands of tourists yearly from the lower cableway station on Tafelberg Road to the mountain top.

The sea is very much a part of Cape Town, and mariners of all nations have looked forward to berthing at the Tavern of the Seas. But it was many years before they could do so in safety, and only from about the mid-19th century was any real progress made on the construction of substantial harbour works. The Victoria and Alfred basins, with the breakwater, are the oldest part of the present harbour, and it is here that the Maritime Museum – rich with relics – is situated. Still a working

ABOVE *Exterior decoration takes many forms, and bands of colour brighten up an otherwise sober structure.*

BELOW *Exuberantly painted decorations of another time and place festoon a restaurant in Waterkant Street.*

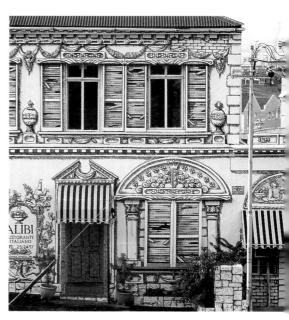

harbour, with trawlers and other craft coming and going and various marine services flourishing on the wharf, the Victoria and Alfred waterfront is also a unique outdoor recreation area, with a brewery, taverns, restaurants, a hotel and a variety of shops. Close by is the fascinating Fort Wynyard military museum, and there is even the opportunity to visit the former Breakwater Prison with its ancient and still-functioning treadmill.

An early and unsuccessful attempt to build a breakwater was made at Mouille Point, where the single-cylinder engine of the steamship *Athens*, wrecked in a gale in 1865, still juts from the sea, close to the shore. From here, houses and blocks of flats line Beach Road in Green Point. The Green Point lighthouse (which Capetonians habitually and perversely refer to as the Mouille Point lighthouse) keeps the steady vigil it has maintained since 1824.

Beyond lies cosmopolitan Sea Point, easily Cape Town's most densely populated suburb, though there are spacious lawns and a promenade where all can enjoy the sea air. As well as people (probably because of them), Sea Point has more restaurants, nightclubs and delicatessens than any other suburb of the Peninsula, offering a variety of different foods – from American-style fast-food to Continental and Oriental cuisine.

From here, curving west and southwards, lie the beaches of what is generally recognized as Cape Town's 'Riviera'. On hot summer days, the white sands at Clifton, Camps Bay and Llandudno are scarcely discernible beneath their over-burden of shapely sun-worshippers. Yachts moor in the clear water just beyond the breakers, and modern apartments – many of them marvels of gravity-defying engineering – cling to the grey, granite slopes of the Twelve Apostles, which form the western face of Table Mountain. Just beyond Llandudno lie the beaches of Sandy Bay, haven of those who love to bare it all.

Victoria Road which follows the coastline all the way from Sea Point, swings briefly inland from Llandudno, before descending to the wooded Hout Bay valley. Yachts and trawlers throng the harbour in the bay, where visitors can enjoy freshly harvested sea-produce at the Fisherman's Wharf. From here, you can gain a view of one of the most impressive marine drives in the world. Chapman's Peak Drive clings to the cliff face, following the line of contact between sandstone and the basement granite. The view back over Hout Bay from the drive is superb, incorporating the bright curve of the beach, the colourful harbour and the sombre sentinel of Hangberg across the glittering waters.

Beyond the peak that gives the scenic drive its name, the long glare of Noordhoek beach comes into view, with the pinnacle that is Slangkop lighthouse in the distance. There was no lighthouse there at the turn of the century, when the master

BELOW RIGHT *Washing lines strung up in the street will often be seen in Woodstock, a suburb where Cape Town's diverse peoples have long lived together.*

BELOW *The Coon Carnival takes to the streets at New Year, and has its origins in the Bo-Kaap, where many of Cape Town's Muslim people have their homes.*

of the brand new steamship, *Kakapo*, made a night-time error of navigation that sent his ship charging high up onto the beach. The boiler and stern post of the ship can still be seen sticking out above the white sand.

The road south heads past Scarborough, Kommetjie, Misty Cliffs and Camel Rock – charming places with charming names – as it rises and falls above the sea, before cutting inland along the northern boundary of the Cape of Good Hope Nature Reserve. This important reserve of almost 8 000 hectares includes some 40 kilometres of coastline, from Schuster's Bay near Scarborough on the Peninsula's western coast to Smitswinkel Bay in the east.

Most visible of the many mammal species that populate the Reserve are the several troops of chacma baboons. Unafraid and impertinent, they stroll about car parks, peer through windscreens and investigate all likely sources of easy food. Visitors are warned not to feed them, as this inevitably leads to their becoming a menace and, sadly, perhaps having to be destroyed. There are many picnic sites and several attractive beaches, each with its own particular mood, within the reserve. The most popular tourist attraction is probably the view site on the high cliffs above Cape Point, with its huge vistas of tossing seas and distant land.

Smitswinkel Bay is a scatter of houses down a steep slope towards a shining white beach. The name is thought to derive from the rocks named Bellows and Anvil just off the shore. Bellows Rock has claimed its share of unwary shipping, most notably the Portuguese liner *Lusitania*, which crashed bows-on into the submerged peril in 1911. Other ships have found safety in Simon's Bay about 10 kilometers further north, especially when the northwest gales of winter made Table Bay unsafe for mooring.

Simon's Town, known affectionately to generations of naval seamen as Snoekie, has been a port for fighting-ships and their attendant vessels since the early 19th century. For many years, this was the base of the South Atlantic Squadron of Britain's Royal Navy and, later, of the South African Navy. A walk along St George's Street, from Jubilee Square to the museum in the old Residency, is a venture into the nautical past.

Here you will also find one end of the Cape Town-Simon's Town railway line, one of the most scenic short train-rides to be found anywhere – between here and Muizenberg the line lies only metres from the rocks and surf. On the way is a stop at Fish Hoek, where an early British governor granted permission for the establishment of a fishery, but forbade the sale of any alcoholic beverage. To this day, faithfully respecting the old edict, Fish Hoek is still 'dry'.

All along this coast you will find pools among the rocks – both natural tidal pools full of tiny, shimmering life forms, and larger man-made ones, laboriously constructed of natural rock, that are favourite bathing places. Young mothers take their children to the sands at St James, where they can watch them paddling in the shallows, or make daring dives off the sea wall back into the calm safety of the pool.

Muizenberg found favour with the mining magnates of the Witwatersrand, and the great imperialist himself, Cecil Rhodes, once owned a house here. Though it was no more than a humble cottage, it was here that he died, and today Rhodes' Cottage is a museum. When Rhodes's architect, Herbert Baker, built his own house here, and called it Sandhills, visitors recorded that they could run from the stoep straight onto the beach. Nowadays, they would probably pause to explore the attractions of the large and colourful pavilion, before proceeding to the seemingly endless sands, where the seemingly endless waves, rank upon rank, march in gentle, stately procession to the beach. It is the comparative warmth of the water at Muizenberg Beach, and indeed at all the beaches along the False Bay coast, that has made this such a popular area for family outings.

False Bay seems a harsh name for these lovely stretches of sand and water, but such it was to the early navigators who, sailing from the east, mistook Hangklip on the eastern side of this bay for Cape Point. The bay can still be seen well inland, from the gracious old homestead of Groot Constantia in the Constantia valley, and it was probably the view that decided Governor Simon van der Stel to build here in 1695. He was a man who loved the Cape and, when he retired from service, he

TOP *With sails like butterfly wings, catamarans wait to take advantage of the breeze.*

ABOVE *A sturdy old wooden fishing boat returns to harbour, trailing a cloud of hungry gulls.*

did not return to live in Holland as most Company officials did, but stayed on at the beloved farm that he called Constantia. The ornamental gables and outbuildings were added by later owners, but the place probably had its present appearance by about 1792, at which time it was owned by one Hendrick Cloete. It was Cloete who had the old wine-cellar built, which sports a magnificently carved pediment attributed to the sculptor Anton Anreith. Constantia wines were famous during the 18th and 19th centuries, and even consoled the Emperor Napoleon in his lonely exile on the Atlantic island of St Helena. Once again, excellent wines – some of the best in the country – are made on the farms of the oak-shaded valley of Constantia, and reach a wide and appreciative market.

Vine-growing had its start in the days of Jan van Riebeeck, close by Constantia on the hill long called Wynberg – the wine mountain. Other crops now occupy a part of his old farmlands, below the craggy eastern face of Table Mountain. Here too lies Kirstenbosch, where the National Botanic Gardens of South Africa have their headquarters. The garden comprises some 828 hectares, of which only 60 are cultivated, the greater part being natural fynbos and forest. More than one fifth of South Africa's flora species grow here, visited by plant-lovers from all over the world. There is a Braille Trail and fragrance garden for the blind, special level walkways for wheelchairs, and a variety of other trails. Winter is the season for proteas, but the gardens blaze with all the glory of daisies and other annuals in spring and early summer.

Kirstenbosch was once part of the vast estate owned by Cecil Rhodes, as was the splendid mountainside setting of the main campus of the University of Cape Town. On a hill above the university is Herbert Baker's temple-like monument to Rhodes, a place of shady pines and picnics, where fallow deer graze quietly and unafraid, and from which both False Bay and Table Bay can be seen. At the foot of the hill is Mostert's Mill, one of the few survivors of the old Dutch-style windmills that were once plentiful, and ground the grain of the colonists.

Wheatlands roll close to the cold waters of the west coast where, from harbours at Saldanha Bay and many small inlets on the arc of St Helena Bay, trawlers and lobster boats set forth, each in their season. Saldanha lies near the mouth of the fabulous Langebaan lagoon, a long stretch of quiet, shallow water that makes a good natural harbour. But for the shortage of fresh water at Saldanha, the Dutch settlement would have been made here, rather than at Table Bay. Now, much of the area is a national park, and hamlets such as Churchhaven dream on in security by the water's edge.

Security was suddenly shattered, one night in 1969, when an earthquake struck the interior, devastating many priceless buildings in the old town of Tulbagh. Its

*ABOVE RIGHT A fruit vendor waits for customers beside his roadside stall in tranquil, shady Noordhoek.*

*BELOW A micro-light aircraft flaunts its bright colours above the long lines of surf.*

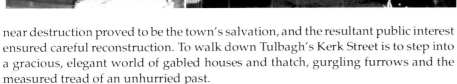

near destruction proved to be the town's salvation, and the resultant public interest ensured careful reconstruction. To walk down Tulbagh's Kerk Street is to step into a gracious, elegant world of gabled houses and thatch, gurgling furrows and the measured tread of an unhurried past.

South of Tulbagh, on the other side the Bain's Kloof Pass, lies the town of Paarl, which derives its name from the huge rock above it that greeted the gaze of an early explorer, glistening with water – like a pearl in the winter sunlight. The headquarters of the Ko-operatieve Wijnbouwers Vereniging (KWV), a statutory body that exercises control over the production of wines and spirits, are found on the 10-kilometre-long main street of this town. Fascinating tours may be undertaken of the organisation's vast cellars, and also of local wine estates. Here, too, you will find the famous Nederburg winery, where an auction of the country's premier wines is held annually.

The wine industry is one of the many attractions of this region, and has its 'capital' at Stellenbosch, a town just to the southwest of Paarl. This is the oldest South African town after Cape Town, established by Governor Simon van der Stel in 1679. The history of the town is very much in evidence as you drive down its oak-shaded streets. All around the town, you will see the vineyards of the Stellenbosch District's wineries, many of which make up the Stellenbosch Wine Route, first of the Cape's wine routes.

Stellenbosch is famous throughout the world for the quality of its wines, which is due in part to the cooling sea breezes that blow in from False Bay to the south, just beyond the towns of Somerset West, Strand and Gordon's Bay. From this last-mentioned town there is a coastal drive that, for scenic beauty, comes close to rivalling the Chapman's Peak road. It leads eastward past the coastal villages of Pringle Bay, Hangklip, Betty's Bay with its magnificent flora reserve, and Kleinmond to Hermanus.

This small but busy coastal town was once called Hermanuspietersfontein, to the despair of postal authorities and locals alike. It has now become a popular resort, and, with a new fishing harbour, a museum in the old harbour, nature reserves and a large, sleepy lagoon, Hermanus has much to offer the visitor who looks for rest in idyllic surroundings.

It is precisely these surroundings which cause the inhabitants of the southwestern Cape, Capetonians in particular, to count themselves lucky to call this far corner of Africa home. Here, they claim, all is within reach that could be desired – sea and mountain, city and countryside. It is a magical mixture, and one to which visitors promise themselves they will return, to explore again, or to uncover some new delight at the friendly old Tavern of the Seas.

ABOVE *The original name of Heerengracht has been restored to the lower portion of Adderley Street. The land here was reclaimed from the sea, which once washed up as far as the Golden Acre building on the left.*

ABOVE LEFT *Work on the Castle of Good Hope began in 1666, it was occupied eight years later and completed in 1679.*

LEFT *The South African Museum is one of several public institutions located within the Company's Gardens, where the first European settlers grew vegetables to supply passing ships.*

PREVIOUS PAGES *The vast basin of Duncan Dock in Table Bay harbour, although no longer the destination of mail-carrying liners plying the waters from Southampton, still provides shelter to ships from all over the world.*

ABOVE *The fruit stalls at the west end of the Grand Parade are an old tradition, though the stalls themselves, with their vague Victorian touches, are relatively new. The Castle garrison exercised regularly on this flat, open piece of ground - hence its name.*

LEFT *Cobbled Greenmarket Square was once the venue at which farmers off-loaded and sold their produce. Today, trading flourishes again, as seemingly countless stall-holders offer a bewildering array of goods to shoppers and tourists.*

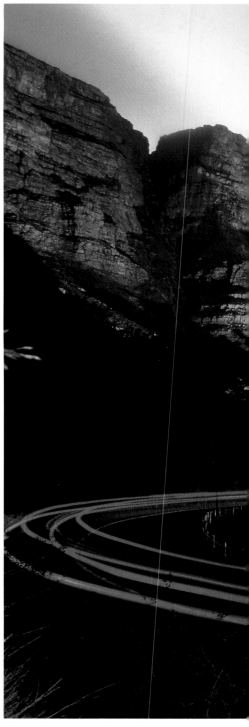

ABOVE *As evening falls, motorists driving along Tafelberg Road see the lights of Cape Town strung out below.*

ABOVE LEFT *Shady pine trees line the Pipe Track, a favourite stroll above the Atlantic-seaboard suburb of Camps Bay.*

LEFT *Seen from the slopes of Signal Hill, wispy cloud spilling over Kloof Nek promises relief from summer heat.*

Attractive developments aimed at providing leisure enjoyment bring new life to the old part of Table Bay Harbour. The Victoria and Alfred Waterfront is the home of hotels, shops, eating-places and also of the fascinating Maritime Museum, which includes floating exhibits. Patrons of Bertie's Landing delight in watching seals clamber from the water to sun themselves on specially constructed platforms. A 'penny ferry' has provided a short cut for many decades, although the tariff has been increased to far beyond the original fare.

LEFT *Steep cobbled streets in the area called Bo-Kaap are lined by attractive little houses with Georgian facades, as well as large and stately mosques.*

RIGHT *Seven kramats, the graves of Muslim holy men, are believed to form a protective circle around Cape Town. Best known of the seven is probably this one atop Signal Hill.*

BELOW *The view from Signal Hill is wide, and this was why a signal-man was stationed here in bygone years. His duty was to warn the Castle of the approach of shipping, a coded system of flags providing information about nationality and type of ship.*

ABOVE *Sea Point's flat-land, under the sugarloaf of Lions' Head, catches the rays of the late afternoon sun. Pockets of sand among the rocks provide tiny, secluded beaches for those who know where to find them, and the bathing pavilion provides recreation for all.*

LEFT *Green Point juts out into the sea, and is the site of South Africa's oldest lighthouse, which was first lit in 1824. Despite the brightness of its beam, several ocean-going vessels have been wrecked almost at its doorstep.*

RIGHT *Sea Point, a crowded and cosmopolitan suburb, boasts more restaurants than any other part of Cape Town.*

ABOVE *Executive-style homes are sprinkled on the slopes above Llandudno. It was known as Kommetjie Bay until a land-owner claimed to detect a resemblance to the Welsh Llandudno early this century. There is only a single access road, and parking, in summer, becomes a pressing problem as holiday-makers flock to the beach.*

LEFT *The jagged-peaked little range that runs above the suburbs of Camps Bay, Bakoven and Llandudno is known as The Twelve Apostles. Early settlers, however, knew it as the Gewelbergen (Gable Mountains).*

PREVIOUS PAGES *Great granite boulders divide the four beaches of Clifton, where yachts often moor in the shallows and bikini-clad bodies soak up the sun.*

ABOVE *The fishing fleet is a feature of Hout Bay's sheltered harbour. Among the vessels anchored here is a floating restaurant, and a retired warship that is open to the public.*

ABOVE RIGHT *The Sentinel, otherwise known as Hangberg, rises from the sea beyond a bright carpet of spring flowers at Hout Bay.*

LEFT *Mariner's Wharf at Hout Bay offers opportunities to sample the fare of the sea, or to browse among nautical curiosities. The bay was named in the 17th century for the profusion of its trees, of which only one small stand remains today.*

ABOVE *Young riders walk their horses in the shallows of Noordhoek's serene and sheltered Long Beach.*

RIGHT *Seen from near Chapman's Peak Drive, Noordhoek's Long Beach is a curve of sparkling white sand that stretches for some eight kilometres to the distant rocky outcrop of Klein-Slangkoppunt. This is a favourite venue for surfers and anglers, although the water is too cold for all but the hardiest swimmers, and there is a particularly strong backwash.*

PREVIOUS PAGES *A feat of engineering and a route of unparalleled splendour, Chapman's Peak Drive hugs the mountain side and offers wide views - of Hout Bay at the northerly end and over the wide, white beach of Noordhoek at the southerly one.*

ABOVE *This is the tip of the Peninsula that Sir Francis Drake described as 'the fairest cape ... in the whole circumference of the earth...'.*

RIGHT *Dias Beach in the Cape of Good Hope Nature Reserve can be reached only by a very steep footpath, preferably at low tide. It lies at the tip of the Peninsula, between Cape Point and the Cape of Good Hope.*

BELOW *Blesbok are among the many animals that roam the Cape of Good Hope Nature Reserve.*

ABOVE *A stroll along St George's Street, from Jubilee Square to the museum in the former Residency, is a walk through history.*

LEFT *Small boats bob on the waters of a peaceful corner of the harbour at Simon's Town, which has been a naval base for almost two centuries.*

LEFT *There's always lively interest - and large crowds - when the fishing boats return to their moorings at Kalk Bay.*

BELOW *On the long, white beach at Fish Hoek, trek-fishing boats are drawn up on the sands. There is no harbour here and the boats are launched from the beach, trailing a net that is held by operators ashore. Paying out net all the way, the boat is rowed in a large 'U' formation, eventually returning to the beach, where the other end of the net is taken ashore. Both ends are then gathered together, and the net hauled in.*

ABOVE *Long lines of breakers make their stately advance towards the gently sloping beach of Muizenberg. Here Rudyard Kipling stayed with his friend Herbert Baker.*

RIGHT *The houses of Marina Da Gama cluster on the far shores of Sandvlei, home to almost all forms of watersport.*

BELOW *Watching for the wave - surfers at Muizenberg have changed the name of the west end of the beach from Neptune's Corner to Surfers' Corner.*

PREVIOUS PAGES *Russet vines of autumn clothe the gentle hills of the Constantia valley, while the gracious homestead of Groot Constantia, its white gables gleaming, dreams on in peace.*

RIGHT *Van der Stel's homestead, in his own lifetime, was known as Constantia, after the quality of constancy, and has indeed been well preserved over the centuries. After his death here in 1712, his great estate was divided and sold, and the major portion received the present name of Groot Constantia.*

BELOW *Among the treasures of Simon van der Stel's old homestead are dishes of rare porcelain, massive furniture in stinkwood and teak, delicate engraved glass and many other items familiar to a gentleman of the early 18th century.*

Kirstenbosch Gardens are the headquarters of National Botanical Gardens of South Africa, established by a resolution of Parliament in 1913. It was once part of the vast Groote Schuur estate bequeathed to the people of South Africa by Cecil Rhodes. A pool with a whimsical bird-like outline is often referred to as Lady Anne Barnard's bath, after the wife of a government official of around 1800, but was probably built by a later owner, Colonel Christopher Bird. Today the Gardens boast between 6 000 and 7 000 indigenous species of plant, providing a blaze of colour to delight the visitor. Sunday breakfast on the terrace, overlooking the gardens, has become a popular pastime with Capetonians.

Mostert's Mill is a prominent roadside landmark beneath Devil's Peak, a part of the Table Mountain massif. Built on the farm Welgelegen ('well situated') in about 1796 by Gijsbert van Reenen, it later passed to his son, Sybrandt Mostert. It fell into disuse for many years, and was finally restored with the help of the Netherlands' government in 1936. In the foreground is the threshing floor, where the hooves of horses separated the grain from the husks and straw. After winnowing, the grain was then ground in the mill. The cap, or roof, can be rotated to set the sails at the most favourable angle to the wind.

ABOVE *The imposing memorial to Cecil Rhodes was designed by his friend and architect, Herbert Baker, to a pattern suggested by the Temple of Zeus in the ancient city of Pergamum in Turkey. An exalted visitor, soon after the the completion of the memorial in 1908, described it as 'the best thing of its kind since the Greeks...' Quite a different atmosphere is created behind the memorial, where a cosy restaurant serves refreshments under the pines.*

LEFT *The spreading campus of the University of Cape Town, with Jamieson Hall as its focal piont, covers ground that once formed part of Cecil Rhodes's Groote Schuur estate. The small white building in the foreground to the left was once the summerhouse of the early Dutch governors.*

ABOVE *With the wind coming in off the sea, a seagull hovers briefly above a bright patch of mesembryanthemums in the Postberg Nature Reserve. The Reserve lies on the isthmus between Langebaan Lagoon and the sea, and forms part of the 20 000-hectare West Coast National Park.*

LEFT *The stark white buildings of the Club Mykonos holiday resort give a Greek-island feel to the small town of Langebaan, where a shallow lagoon is separated from the sea by the narrow Postberg peninsula.*

RIGHT *A rare (and expensive) delicacy is the Cape rock lobster (*Jasus lalandii*). Fishermen of the village of Paternoster show some of their catch.*

ABOVE *Zebra in the Postberg Nature Reserve pause in their grazing as they tread a spring carpet of briefly blooming flowers. The Reserve also boasts animals such as eland, kudu, springbok, lynx and ostrich.*

LEFT *The shores of Langebaan lagoon are alive with the colour of myriad flowers in spring and early summer. This large and tranquil sheet of water attracted settlers centuries ago, and along its shores are a few historic old homesteads and the tiny village of Churchhaven.*

RIGHT *The west coast as far to the north as Namaqualand is a colourful paradise for a few short weeks in spring, as many brighly coloured flowers thrust up from the sandy soil.*

ABOVE *Paarl was the birthplace of the group that called itself Die Genootskap van Regte Afrikaners (the society of true Afrikaners). They were largely responsible for promoting Afrikaans as an acceptable language, and their achievement was honoured a century later by the unveiling of the Taalmonument (language monument) on the outskirts of Paarl.*

RIGHT *The three great granite rocks of Paarl, when seen for the first time by a European, were glistening like jewels with morning dew. That, at any rate, was the impression of the Dutch explorer, who named them 'the mountains of diamonds and pearls'. Below lies the picturesque town of Paarl, home of the KWV.*

ABOVE *First granted in 1713, Boschendal had developed, a century later, into its present magnificent form as one of the classics of Cape Dutch architecture. The ground-floor plan of the homestead is that of an H, and it stands at the head of two parallel rows of outbuildings. Open to the public, Boschendal still produces fine wines.*

LEFT *The mountains of Groot Drakenstein rear up behind the vineyards of the Boschendal Estate, situated between the towns of Stellenbosch and Franschhoek.*

ABOVE *Vineyards and windbreaks of pine and gum make patterns on the floor of the Franschhoek valley, where Huguenot families, refugees from religious persecution in France, were settled in 1688.*

RIGHT *Set amid lawns and flower gardens, the soaring Huguenot Monument is composed of three lofty arches representing the Holy Trinity of Christianity. A sun of righteousness rises above the central arch, and is topped by a cross. In front stands the sculpture of a woman, her feet on a globe of the earth, representing freedom of conscience. The monument was unveiled in 1948.*

*Woodland and vineyards cover the valleys and mountain slopes near Stellenbosch, an area first settled by European farmers in 1679. The area is one of the most scenic of the southwestern Cape, and a popular tourist attraction.*

LEFT *The outdoor setting of the amphitheatre at Oude Libertas in Stellenbosch lends a special atmosphere to evening performances of dance, drama and song.*

RIGHT *A stroll down Stellenbosch's oak-lined Dorp Street is a walk into an earlier and more gracious era of stately, gabled dwellings.*

BELOW *Oom Samie se Winkel is a throwback to the general dealer of times past, where the visitor will be confronted with an extraordinary array of goods – from old-fashioned sweets and chewing tobacco to calabashes and leather whips.*

ABOVE *To ensure the highest quality in wine, grapes are picked by hand on the farms around Stellenbosch. Here, pickers on the farm Rustenburg, bring in the harvest.*

ABOVE RIGHT *The Stellenbosch Wine Route is a popular tourist attraction, especially with those wishing to sample the wines of the Cape, and the cellar at Delheim provides a pleasant atmosphere for tasting.*

LEFT *The museum at Stellenbosch Farmers' Winery has preserved the implements of wine-making from days gone by, when the scale of operations was much smaller – and the process much simpler.*

ABOVE *Yachts lie in the harbour of Gordon's Bay, an inlet on the eastern curve of False Bay.*

RIGHT *Tumbling breakers and a strong backwash are features of the sea at Koeël Bay.*

BELOW *There are several stud farms in the vicinity of Somerset West.*

OVERLEAF *The immense variety of shrubby Cape fynbos found between Kleinmond and Hermanus forms part of one of the most prolific floral kingdoms in the world.*

*At the old harbour at Hermanus,*
*fishing boats long retired from the sea*
*still point their prows towards a quiet*
*Indian Ocean.*